Contents

George Washington

Josh's Day 3
Fiction

A Great Man 11
Nonfiction

HOUGHTON MIFFLIN   BOSTON

Copyright © 2008 by Houghton Mifflin Company. All rights reserved.

No part of this work may be reproduced or transmitted in any form or by any means, electronic or mechanical, including photocopying or recording, or by any information storage or retrieval system without the prior written permission of Houghton Mifflin Company unless such copying is expressly permitted by federal copyright law. Address inquiries to School Permissions, Houghton Mifflin Company, 222 Berkeley Street, Boston, MA 02116.

Printed in China

ISBN-13: 978-0-618-93228-3
ISBN-10: 0-618-93228-3

1 2 3 4 5 6 7 8 9 SDP 15 14 13 12 11 10 09 08

Words to Know

stand   camps
tents   damp
went   Gramps

field

Story Words

president

Josh's Day

by Dennis Fertig
illustrated by David Wenzel

It is a damp day. A big crowd is in town. They came to see George Washington. He will pass through town soon.

"Washington is on his way to start his job," said Gramps. "He will be the first president of the United States."

"Half the town is here," said Josh.

"People came from far away, too," said Gramps. "Men set up camps in fields and slept in tents."

Kids had boxes to stand on in the crowd.

"Will I see him?" said Josh.
"You will," Gramps said.
George Washington is close,
but Josh cannot see him yet.

"I can lift you up," said Gramps.
Now Josh can see a tall man on a white horse. The man sees Josh and waves to him.

"I saw George Washington as he went by!" said Josh. "He saw me, too!"

Words to Know

think strong
king things
long

war field

Story Words

president

A Great Man

by Dennis Fertig

We live in the United States. A long, long time ago, a king ruled here. He lived in a land far, far away.

11

People did not think about the king at first. After a while, they did not want a king to be in charge.

The king liked to keep things the same. He sent soldiers to tell people that he would not change. People did not like this, so a war started here.

The people had a good man to help them win the war. He led the troops through fields and towns to fight the soldiers. It took a long time, but the people did win!

The man who helped win was strong and brave. He was George Washington. Now, people had to pick a strong and brave man to be president.

WASHINGTON'S INAUGURATION AS PRESIDENT.

The people chose George Washington to be in charge. He was our first president!